# This Country of Mothers

CRAB ORCHARD AWARD SERIES IN POETRY

# This Country of Mothers

JULIANNA BAGGOTT

*Crab Orchard Review*

*&* Southern Illinois University Press

Carbondale and Edwardsville

The Crab Orchard Award Series in Poetry is a joint publishing
venture of Southern Illinois University Press and *Crab Orchard
Review.* This series has been made possible by the generous support
of the Office of the President of Southern Illinois University and the
Office of the Vice Chancellor for Academic Affairs and Provost at
Southern Illinois University Carbondale.

**Crab Orchard Award Series in Poetry Editor: Jon Tribble
Judge for 2000: Rodney Jones**

Text design by Erin Kirk New

Library of Congress Cataloging-in-Publication Data

Baggott, Julianna.
This country of mothers / Julianna Baggott.
p. cm.—(Crab Orchard award series in poetry)
1. Mothers—Poetry. 2. Mothers and daughters—Poetry.
I. Title. II. Series.
PS3552.A339 T48 2001        00-058794
811'.6—dc21
ISBN 0-8093-2381-8 (paper : alk. paper)

To my mother, Glenda, and my daughter, Phoebe.

There is no invention to it, there is no trick, there is no fake;

you simply lie down in a coffin and breathe quietly.

—HARRY HOUDINI

I long for blood, the womb's salty heaven,

to break from the sack and push my skull

up to the light like a green shoot, to be

an egg candled to see if its soul exists.

# Contents

# Acknowledgments

I would like to thank the following publications where these poems first appeared:

*American Literary Review* — "Dear Mr. Houdini,"

*The Chattahoochee Review* — "The Beginning" and "What We Didn't Talk about at Fifteen"

*Crab Orchard Review* — "Learning to Say No at the Immaculate Conception High School" and "The Assumption: Mary's Heart in the *Guinness Book of World Records*"

*Cream City Review* — "The Cold War: My Parents as Newlyweds" and "The Extra Rib"

*CutBank* — "Conception" and "My Mother Prays to Dream of Her Dead Father"

*Green Mountains Review* — "Satisfying the God of Statistics"

*Indiana Review* — "Checkup after the Operation to Evacuate the Dead Fetus"

*The Laurel Review* — "The Dead Must Disappear or Join a Story"

*Ms. Magazine* — "The Annunciation: Our Mothers at Church"

*Nimrod* — "Cesarean"

*North Dakota Quarterly* — "How I Fear God"

*Notre Dame Review* — "After Eleven Days of Rain"

*Poet Lore* — "My Daughter, like Eve, Realizes Nakedness"

*Poetry* — "How It Begins"

*Quarterly West* — "The Knocking Tree"

*River Styx* — "What I Told the Jehovah's Witness" and "Seventy Degrees in December"

*Southern Poetry Review* — "Living Where They Raised Me"

*The Southern Review* — "After Giving Birth, I Recall the Madonna and Child," "My Mother among Bears," "Blurbs," "Nights in Tijuana," and "What the Poets Could Have Been"

*Spoon River Poetry Review* — "Preschool" and "The Cow Remembers Urus"

*Sundog: The Southeast Review* — "Kitchens: 1959"

*The Virginia Quarterly Review* — "My Cousin Attempts Suicide in Gander Hill Prison" and "My Mother's *National Geographics*"

*West Branch*—"Correcting Memory," "Recalling the Leg" and "First Time"
*Willow Springs*—"Discussing Sorrow with Jesus" and "Mother as
  Judas"

I would also like to thank Fleda Brown, Rachel Pastan, Linda Pastan,
Marisa DelosSantos, Mariano Espiritu, Katherine Varnes, James
Keegan, Anne Colwell, and Lenae Nofciger for all of their care and
help. Thanks also to the Virginia Center for the Creative Arts, the
Ragdale Foundation, Bread Loaf Writers' Conference, and Delaware
Division of the Arts, especially Barbara King. I would like to give a
special thanks to Fred Chappell and Andrew Hudgins for their
encouragement. And I cannot forget the boys: thanks to my husband,
David G. W. Scott, my first teacher of poetry; to my father, Bill Baggott;
and to my sons, Finneas and Theo.

# One

## How It Begins

That spring when my parents' bodies were still pristine
and the sex so new that each time they were dazed,
grinning like kids holding sparklers in the dark —

can she recall that giving in, knees first,
the ground folding beneath her, how only then
she began to know fear, that it tallies up beat for beat

with love and the world can betray us because we finally
want something from it? For her it was the do-gooders
always claiming the most common things will kill us —

furnace pipes asbestos-wrapped, pesticide-sprayed grapes,
even tap water radiated. And she began to wash her hands,
trying to keep clean, to risk nothing; she became a genius,

inventing the patterned travel of germs, from hand to mouth
to vital organ and the lazy swirling ones that love to linger
in towels and sink drains, how detergent itself was lethal.

She scrubbed for us, each plate and spoon, her hands
cracked and bleeding; she boiled and boiled our meat.
I've decided it is a sweetness no one deserves, her love

for us grown too large, like the oversized heart ever expanding
to compensate for one weak murmuring valve,
and the weakness too is love, a constant falling.

# Kitchens: 1959

The year Nixon showed up in Moscow
in front of Macy's Model Kitchen and finger-poked

Khrushchev's broad chest, my mother lost her first baby.
Russians crowded the railed-off kitchen,

a display of modern American living.
Imagine the potato-and-onion smell of so many wool coats,

the cupboard hanging open to show off shelf space,
the box of S.O.S. ready to scrub it all down.

When Khrushchev says to Nixon in his husky Russian tongue,
*Go fuck my grandmother,* Elliot Erwitt translates the street talk,

shoots frame after frame that I'll find later in a book:
two angry men and the kitchen so small and tidy, I can only think

of my mother's first kitchen, her view the same as Erwitt's
if she'd been sitting at the breakfast table

in the garage apartment on Fernwood Street in Portsmouth,
a military town where they roll the mattresses

up on the beds because of the bugs,
but this one's not bad: a ceramic sink,

a Frigidaire, and a Hot Point stove for $75 a month.
My father's in his last year of duty,

the Russians are winning the final frontier,
and the A-bomb could drop from the sky

and melt every house on Fernwood Street,
but for now my mother is puffy and pale.

The bleeding started fast, the tiny child
lost in it somewhere—she never saw

what she'd imagined: arms, legs, her own small face—
and now days later, she shuffles to the cold stove.

It's on the blink, a wire coil model;
one little wire overheated and the whole thing shut down.

She turns it off, reaches in, fingers the wires,
twist-ties them. She's got a meat loaf

from a neighbor on the counter.
In a week or two she'll see the campaign poster

at the grocery store, Nixon and Khrushchev chin to chin.
She'll vote for Nixon, thinking maybe one day

his toughness will save her, her husband,
the small cluster of eggs inside her.

But she has already begun to doubt things.
She thinks nothing is truly reliable, not her body,

not this easy American life. She starts up the oven,
and as the wires solder themselves,

my mother smells smoke; something small is burning.

## Conception

I will collapse beneath this tender task,
keeping the record, the sun-stroked mantel clock,

the chipped soup bowl, the hum of the dome hair dryer
pouring heat from its dim sky of little holes.

My parents are making love in early spring,
late in the day while her grandmother, up for a visit,

sits at the dining room table, lifts the empty bowl
to her lips again and again, deaf

under the blue helmet—her hair drying
to an electric rise. I am swelling

and waiting, a ticking egg, a twisting tail,
a fly smashing against bright glass.

I imagine my mother's quiet breath in his ear,
his hands, blood-swollen from the metal grooves

and sharp-toothed gears in the motor pool, and Jesus
hung above the bed, head lolled

as if to get a better angle on their lovemaking,
a witness to all he missed. His wooden cross

trembles against the flowered wall.
Outside the window, a bird bobs on a branch,

a dog barks, a kid on skates clatters
down the sidewalk like a tin train,

and the daffodils give the first yellow twists
within their thick green tongues.

# The Cold War: My Parents as Newlyweds

If the Russians pushed the red button,
my parents were to meet at a corner store

where Route One intersected Route Three,
toward Culpeper. My father was at ground zero;

he could see the White House from his window
in the patent office where he poured over

anything cleaned by air, the cotton mills'
ceiling-track vacuum cleaners,

giant street sweepers, even my mother's
hand-held Hoover. They both knew

he'd never make it out of the downtown traffic,
and so she was only to wait half an hour

before heading west. She'd get the news
by radio in their new Arlington apartment,

pack the German Luger that her father had pried
from a dead enemy soldier, a family heirloom,

and a lockbox of cash, hidden in my father's sock drawer.
They kept the car tanked with gas, bottled water, maps.

I was a scab in her womb, something she was willing
to sacrifice. Years later she told me

she never intended to make it past the corner store.
She would wait forever, till the sky turned to red ash.

## My Mother Gives Birth

They gave her a form of truth serum,
not to dull the pain, to dull memory.
But she does remember
asking the nurse to take off her girdle—
not a girdle but her skin taut with pain—
that the nurse told her to stop screaming,
the girl one over was having her first
and scared enough already.
She rolled my mother to her side, standard procedure,
handcuffed her to the bed rails, left her to labor alone.
My mother says her last thought was of Houdini,
that she too could fold the bones of her hands
and escape. I want her to slip free,
to rise up from her bed and totter
out of that dark ward of moaning women.
I want to be born in black dirt.
But her mind went white as cream lidding a cup.
And she does not remember,
although her eyes were open, blank,
how I spun from her body, wailing,
drugged for truth, my wrists on fire.

# Two

## Correcting Memory

I don't want to know. Our cheeks were pink,
our knees like wax fruit never bruised.

Our mothers chirped like birds and our fathers
kept map-folded handkerchiefs in their back pockets.

We rowed wooden boats to school
and caught fish with our bare teeth.

Don't you remember how the houses
always smelled of fresh fried fish

and the apple trees, oh, their chimney-sized trunks
and how the limbs, weighted with bright bobs,

grew into open windows, our fathers snow-struck with blossoms,
our mothers vacuuming paths through the petals and seeds?

No, you must tell me. I already know the man.
I can see him by the tracks that parted town like paired eels.

Why was everything always wet, clothes unpinned
from the line still damp and sheets always sticking to skin?

One large hand burrowed deep in soiled pants, he fed rocks
to the stray dog, flipped them up and watched it snap.

Was he heavy? The stones sharp in your flexed back?
Eyes clenched, the bright world turned to the death-rot of leaves

and wet newspaper where rats chewed nests.
And where were our parents?

The basement ceilings were cluttered with sturdy pipes,
the closets dark thickets of leather belts.

Today I looked over a schoolyard of children
and tried to remember the color of your hair.

But, again and again, I was stolen by the stray dog,
matted fur, belly weighted with stones.

Sometimes I find the dog at the bottom of a creek bed
pinned to slick clay. When I swim to the surface, alone,

and stagger waterlogged into the woods,
no matter how far, I can still hear its moan.

## The Knocking Tree

When I complain about the skinny tree
with no blooms knocking all night

against the clapboard shingles,
you offer to cut it down, adding

that its roots in time will undermine
the cinder-block foundation.

But I was once an ugly girl,
treelike in my knotted joints,

with yellow skin as if taken
by cottonrust, a ruderal child, confined

to back brace, picking weathered shed wood
as steam rose from winter laundry

clipped to line. I've told you
how each night, while darkness like couch grass

covered the hissing roadside weeds,
I waited on the edge of an iron-framed bed

for my mother to unbuckle the brace.
I have wanted to say to someone

all my life what I still cannot say to you
even now as the brace turns on an attic hook

like a cicada's husk, something born from its broken spine:
*Slip your hand beneath the dark corset; it's so soft*

*that later, when rubbing your fingers together,*
*you will feel the wet pollen of my other skin.*

## Recalling the Leg

At thirteen, I was afraid
of my grandfather's fake leg,
hairless and pink, black sock
and shiny shoe, the way it appeared
suddenly, propped in the closet
amid galoshes, or leaning casually
against a wall like part of a cocksure
lover I might have one day,
and too like loss.

I imagine him running the wounded
to sterile tents, his hands clamped
on the stretcher, soldiers' boots
bobbling at his chest and then
as if hit by a gusted boom, thrown
to the worn field where bloated
cows rotted, hooves reaching—
and his leg, scattered clumps
of wet red flowers sun-polished.

Some nights, I turn on each light
till the house burns to search
for the restless boy my husband becomes
in dreams, shooing daddy's chickens
to pen. Tonight, I find him curled
beneath my mother's metal tea tray,
so meticulous, so perfect,
soft knot of jaw, fine curling hairs,
bare foot arched glistening in light,
he shocks me, the whole of him,
flushed with sleep, not lifelike
but alive, not the poem,
but that first bright cock in my hand.

# Nights in Tijuana

*for Jack*

At twelve, my cousin had romantic fever,
something torrid and hot
                like night
in our imagined Tijuana
where everyone fell in love.
While his joints swelled and the valves
of his heart gave,
           just a little, he remembered
our collected fireflies
caught earlier that summer in a glowing glass jar,
how they lit his father's atlas map,
                  Tijuana,
the tiny embers of their hearts
already, again, and then still burning.

His father blamed the fever
for his softness.
          And he agreed.
It was the first fitful dream
of the exotic,
         the men he would love.

He went to Tijuana years later
and brought me trinkets
of Jesus, tiny medallions
that shone, a glint of gold in his palm.
He knew he was dying,
steering clear of his father's shame
and his mother, who couldn't bear
to lose him again, to this,
what could not be love.
           He told me it was

the opened mouths,
        the giving over
of bodies, it was
       sometimes
just as we had imagined it would be,
nights in Tijuana
just before falling in love,
his life,
     a dream between fevers.

## Learning to Say No at the Immaculate Conception
## High School

For years they only taught us to bend
                              at the waist,
to kneel and bow our heads, but our bodies
arched
      naturally like blades of wet grass
when knees were weak and heads
                        heavy with wanting.
Inside his Pop's Wagoneer parked by the tracks—
the train's one-eye
bearing down, the press of it so solitary
and blinding—
            under Jimmy Vetrie's gaze,
how could I say anything?
Why would I want to,
after all of those aching sentences
                        about geometry
and his brother's sleeper hold?
Finally, pale,
            we stretched against each other.
And they kept it up, filmstrips
of dirty loveless girls
                  and how to shake
our heads until it became a breath,
a whisper,
        until our hips rang with it,
*no, no, no,* as mechanical as the train's churn
and above it
        the whistled moan rising.

## First Time

The motel clerks were deformed, slow witted,
with hands shriveled
                          up into their arms.
On my back, I thought of their blunt boiled bodies
and a certain polio-stricken nun
                              leaning on wrist-clasp canes
who told me once in a gym's thick dust,
*When you take your vows, you dress like a bride*
*because you are marrying Jesus.*
I imagined Jesus
                    on their wedding night
lifting the long white skirt,
                              her pale twisted legs,
the metaphor playing out in a sexual miracle
that didn't take.
                    I thought of my own uterus,
tight and small as a pear, the broken seal of it,
and what could now take root,
                              stumped arms, bowed legs,
the squalling mouth and hollow head
of a sinful child, and again of the nun's skirt,
                                        its secret folds,
how everything had its place — tiny scissors, a file,
the rosary slung
                    from one unseen hitch to another, how
if I could have asked her where she kept her desire,
she would have patted a secret compartment
of her long dark habit and smiled,
                              whispering, *Right here.*
But I never asked. I slipped out one night
after the head count, down the hall, following
the clipped field
                    to the sighing highway's tall grass

and waited
            for a pair of headlights to slow,
a door to pop open, a hand
                        to help hoist me into a truck
and how it happened, a real truck, a real hand.
Later, the clerks blinked, one plucked the key
with a hammer-shaped thumb and finger
and slipped it
            onto a hook in a little box
drilled to the wall.
That is what I remember most clearly:
rows and rows
            of hooks and keys and numbers.

# What We Didn't Talk about at Fifteen

*for Elsbeth*

We never spoke of the drowned girl,
found naked and raped. Flashlights stuttered
through trees until one lit her body
tangled in lake grass
and everything continued on:
we filed past the empty desk,
crowded the row of bathroom mirrors,
but I want to know, years later,
if we all secretly imagined the stirred silt
rising around her
like our mothers' powder, sunstruck,
and the shy girl's mouth and eyes
open wide as if she'd died
singing our favorite radio song,
*sugar, sugar, oh.*
Didn't each of our mothers warn
it could have been us? And the man,
still alive and stalking,
didn't we all harbor him;
don't we still wake up some nights
running beside the tall lake grass?
Didn't her death wean us from childhood
the way some factory women
claimed to wean their babies,
nipples coated in hot sauce,
a live coal in the mouth?
And didn't we all fall in love
with her; spend these years
hoping to find her one day,
sitting quietly at a bank teller's desk,
still young, how we would hold her,
rock her, singing sweetly.

## My Mother Refuses to Wear Glasses

Vanity would be a fine excuse
or even safekeeping, if thought so fragile
she had hidden them—her glasses folded, thin arms
crossing oversized eyes
like a child pretending to angel-sleep.
But she isn't vain or precious.
She's bought the dime-store varieties
with flimsy chains. One by one
she lets them disappear, left behind
at restaurant tables, by department store check-outs,
in between fabric bolts at the piece goods shop.
I have decided it is a chosen ignorance,
a repeated denial of the slick bright focus,
to see each leaf standing alone
from the others, that she prefers
a desperate world, emerging and retreating,
the road bending toward shadow,
each path on the verge
of revealing itself.
                    Sometimes, she admits,
she thinks of the night
her mother took her to the convent's dark door,
because her father was angry and drunk.
She knows now that he went looking for them,
cruising southern highways, illiterate and lost,
passing road sign after road sign,
the whole world trying to tell him something
if only he could make it out.
Somewhere he broke as he always did,
the flash gone from his eyes,
suddenly teary, blinking, too wide,
and Johnny Law brought him home
in the back seat of a cruiser,
but she was waiting for him at the convent window,

the sick mix of love and hate,
for the hero, the villain.
Sometimes, even now with him dead for years,
she can look up the street, and, without glasses,
every narrow-boned man
at a distance can be her father,
pale and exhausted, just before
he sees her, just before
the first register of relief, just before
he breaks into an open-armed run.

## My Grandfather Returns after Many Years

Like the saints who walked to the city
from their open tombs when Jesus rose,
he is surprised to find himself here,
the small sawing of breath in his throat,
the way it all goes on without him.

My mother lets him watch her scrub the sink,
wipe a waxy apple on her skirt,
wheel the milk carton from one Dixie cup
to the next—a show of her patience
for the everyday battle, to say,

I am not you. I was born
from a bed, springs groaned,
the mattress heaved, and I appeared
at the headboard, already tucked in.
And yet she still believes she could have stopped him

if she hadn't been so loud, swallowed coins,
thrown goose shit at the shed,
if she hadn't worn him down and through
like a hat to the bare band, like a memory
rubbed so clean it is no longer true.

At the kitchen table, she tells him the story
of how once as a child the family fell asleep
with no electric, and in the middle of the night
the ceiling fan began to whir,
the television lit up and spoke,

the refrigerator found its tongue,
clicked and hummed like a miraculous healing,
how he took her by the hand and told her
they were ghosts in the house of the living.
It's all she wants to remember, but his face is vacant.

# How I Fear God

My mother shoveled up the carpet of grass,
flipping it to an earthen underbelly,
and stroked the loose dirt as if it were a bear,
its fine hair of roots uncoiling beneath her hand,
the crumbled dirt collecting at her knees.
I squatted beside her, looking for the purple twists of worms.
As she dug the hole, she said the smell
reminded her of her father, the grave digger.
*How many times,* my mother asked, *did the old man
wonder if he was digging the grave for himself?*
I thought of my grandfather asleep inside the house,
his fluttering lids and silent pill-stained tongue,
the white of his bones shining beneath his skin
thin as a worn Bible page, his head crowned
in late afternoon light. She lifted the tree from a bag
and placed its bald roots into the hole.
When the tree stood solidly in the ground,
my mother sent me in to tell him to take a look.
The streetlights shone like a row of moons;
the junked-up field was filled with gold-eyed raccoons.
I called for him, running from room to room—
the empty bed, the glowing bedside milk glass
gone blue, the walls clicking with mice—
until breathless I stumbled into the dark kitchen.
He'd been there all along, leaning
against the kitchen sink, watching from the window,
licking salt from his cupped palm.

## Coming Home at Seventeen

In his father's roadster, I remember
our exposed radio-lit bones,
                              our pearly oils
tinged red with blood,
how the car, sealed shut, filled with steam
so like a bathroom pumped with hot shower water
I could only think
of my mother,
                rocking me on the tub's edge,
my throat constricted with midnight croup,
each cough ringing my ribs,
my own voice
        an animal bark and moan,
until slowly my throat opened again,
my body went slack
                        with something near sleep,
my hand a tiny pink star
                        on her sagging breast.
He drove me home past unwashed churches,
seam-rusted silos, a man caught in his headlights,
shoveling a raccoon from the roadside.
At home, I stood in her flower patches,
name-tagged like school children,
white plastic posts marked with laundry pen.
The basement's bare bulb
                        shined through the window wells;
and the dark house, belly-lit,
seemed to hover
                just above earth like a spaceship.
My father lingered underground,
wide fingertips running over
the greased gears of his clocks.
Through the open upstairs windows,

where curtains billowed like veils,
                                        I could hear my mother
from their bed, calling his name, calling.
I waited for the house to heave from earth
in a whir
                of clipped grass and shingles,
dust-ruffles and splintered wood.
My father pulled the chain
                        on the basement bulb,
and turned on the front porch light—
in the slow dilation of morning
                                it burned
like a golden pear, like fruit on fire.

## My Mother's *National Geographic*s

Our house tilted forward, an errant tooth in the row,
because my heavy mother, the neighbors joked,

sat nose-pressed to the window,
staring out at the street, the children

with broomstick handles and halved tennis balls,
and, perhaps, into the dim red-fringed windows

of the lantern-strung Dragon's Den, the Chinoiserie,
where couples leaned together in the dull glow.

The mailman was a whistler.
She could hear him two blocks down

and met him at the door.
When the *National Geographic* arrived each month,

she put it in a wicker basket next to the toilet
with its dreamy bright blue water,

and she'd stack the old one in the attic, neatly,
the pile rising each month like a child, by quarter inches.

I never saw her read them,
but she must have flipped through pages:

the veiled Bedouin, Tibetan women hauling timber
like crosses on their shoulders,

and the Gimi men in gourd masks
sticking their tongues through pigs' teeth.

Did she imagine her life splayed
in captioned photographs: The female of the tribe

taking a pot from the stove, ladling beans
and chopped dogs onto plates?

Would they have said she seemed invisible,
that we grunted into our food?

Once, she slapped my father, pleading,
*Talk to me.* He said nothing, steam rising

from the beans to his red cheek
like a Raji at the base of a bus-sized tree trunk

where he has lowered hive after hive
and now sits stunned from bee poison,

the roar of a million angry wings in his ears,
and my mother by the sink, wept

like a Raji woman wringing honey from a comb.

# The Annunciation: Our Mothers at Church

Every year it became clearer:
                              Gabriel stooping to flattery,
like any man in a honky-tonk bar
                              after midnight.
He doesn't use the conditional, all future-tense,
although it is a question,
                    isn't it?
And what about Mary,
                angling
without insult,
              the virgin wondering
how the child wouldn't come from rape?
When she said yes again each year,
                              our mothers, teetering
on the wooden pew's edge,
                        sighed a little,
a small death in their lungs.
They wished, for once,
                    she would say no,
that someone would finally say no.
But she is the handmaid of the Lord,
                              her knuckles raw
like their own
              from scrubbing sins,
and for a moment they closed their eyes,
and remembered
              those broad beating wings,
                              the feathered light,
and then, how quickly,
                the angel was gone.

# Three

# After Giving Birth, I Recall the Madonna and Child

Who could ever believe it:
    the cows, shoulder to shoulder,
        lowing three-part harmony,
the stable so Hollywood-set tidy,
Joseph and Mary, serene, smiling,
and the boy, pink and fat, already blessing us
        with two tiny fingers raised
from his white swaddle?

He's never purple, blood-stained,
        yellowed—like my babies—
        from swimming in his own shit.

Maybe if we could see her belly
hardened by contraction,
        her knees
            spread, steam rising
from the wash of blood,
and her face contorted with pain,
the cords of her neck
        taut and blue,
then we might believe Joseph,
how he must have said,
        *I can see the head.*
            *It's glowing.*

# First Pregnancy

I could not believe a child.
Instead, I envisioned a landscape,
an ocean turning in on itself,
a moving mountain, a field

that could fold and unfold,
my body overtaken by a living map.
Even once when her hand appeared
from the other side—

a five-fingered hand print
as clear as a preschooler's plaster mold—
I could not accept the benediction.
Like Thomas, I am hard-hearted.

I need the body, to watch Jesus
eat the white fish,
pick his teeth with its bones,
my hands caked in his blood.

## Satisfying the God of Statistics

I still prefer the children of strangers,
Girl Drowns in Back Yard Pool,
Boy Slugged by Neighbor's Handgun,
the evening news camera panning
a cabin of leukemia-stricken campers.
But in the early years, their veins
etched under soft skin, the heartbeat
pulsing on the soft centers of their heads,
I was capable of anything.
My husband's friend told me
his newborn's head was the size of a tennis ball,
and then he corrected himself, no, a plum.
I couldn't stop the sinful incantation:
Thank God not mine, Thank God not mine.
I placed the limp dishrag on the sink's bent neck,
listened to the tap of the faucet
and my daughter upstairs speaking
in the tiny voices of dolls as she fell asleep.
I don't believe it works this way,
but I cannot stop searching the thickets
for the ugly ram, horns wrapped in thorned vines—
how many times did I erect the altar
in that thankful sigh, place the head in my palm,
wrap someone else's child in ropes,
and pick up the glinting knife?

# Preschool

The teacher matches child to mother—Alexis to the tanned blonde
in argyle socks and khaki shorts; Harley, in his blue paper hat,
to the woman with fish earrings. It's the way I'd imagined birth,
the presentation of a chatty child with teeth and hair,

how Little Red Riding Hood, holding granny's hand,
stepped from the wolf's gut in her shiny black shoes,
the two of them polished by the gullet, surprised, new, whole.
I am not the wolf but the woodcutter, leaning proudly on his ax.

The teacher glances at me, then back into the classroom.
She hands me a little sweater with dirty cuffs
and the child that goes with it.
Of course, I'd recognize her anywhere,

sticky cheeks, rumpled hair, eyes too big for the head,
and the newspaper hat overflowing with glitter and gold wire.
I kneel, whisper, "Mama, how I've missed you.
Will you hold my hand?" It fits, a tiny white vase in my palm.

## Seventy Degrees in December

1.

We've grown accustomed to death,
but today in warm wind
        the leaves clamber
to return to their limbs—
not from regret as much as confusion.
And I am pregnant again.
This baby I already know,
        stitching itself
inside me, something desperate.
I imagine its birth feet first
ready to steel itself against gravity.
My grandmother believes that bees
are the souls of the dead,
that dead souls
        are folded, like eggs
with cake batter, into the infant body or before.
Bees dream of the tulip's sweet cradle.
I pull down a bare limb.
It is covered
        with impossible buds.

2.

We never grow accustomed to death,
        leaves, perhaps
but not the baby dying in the womb.
Wasn't I the desperate one, steeling myself
against birth?
        My grandmother is here again,
this time not with her bees
but to tell me Aunt Effie lost one this way too,
so long inside her, though,
        it turned to stone.

I imagine that is the weight
that stays in my belly,
                a rock child that could fit
in the palm of my open hand.
And what of the bare limbs?
Did I expect the impossible buds to bloom?

# Checkup after the Operation to Evacuate the Dead Fetus

We all want comfort.
Monsieur Lotito holds a record
in the *Guinness Book,*
eating two-and-a-half pounds of metal and glass a day:
eighteen bikes, seven TVs,
        a coffin, once,
handles, hinges and all.
Mrs. H swallowed bent pins—
        how the pricks
must have let her know
that all inside her
        was alive.
The doctor asks how I am;
I answer, *I must have bit my lip,*
        *a sore spot twitches*
*each time I pass over it with my tongue,*
*and I cannot stop tonguing it.*
Any bleeding? Cramping? *No,* I say, *no.*
*You vacuumed very well, delicately. You'd have made*
*an excellent and thorough housewife.*
I'm the only one who laughs.
I'm guilty
    not quite of throwing my child into water
to teach it to swim,
        but close,
guilty of not knowing the moment
it drowned,
    of feeling it roll
and pitch, swearing it alive
when clearly it was not.
And, yes, if you must know,
I missed my taut stomach,
my husband's hand stretched from nipple
to nipple,

a perfect octave apart,
that it was my third child,
one every other year,
    and I cried
when I found I was pregnant,
that, yes, I am to blame;
      it died
because I didn't want it enough,
and how do I live with that?
I don't tell the doctor, the prim nurse
that on my kitchen table,
    a pomegranate sits,
its tough rind cut in half,
      its pulp tight
with a hundred shiny pulsing hearts.
I would eat it whole. I say,
*I'm fine, doing well. Can I go now?*

## You Found Me in the Dry Tub, Fevered, Whispering of God

After the miscarriage, you tore up the bathroom floor,
tacky linoleum layers, asbestos tiles;
you unscrewed tub faucets, pipe panels,
looking for a leak, a trail
                              of damage to its source,
but water is tricky. It can run from room to room
along unseen beams.
                     Finally you gave up, headed out
through snow-bent orchard limbs, for miles.
From bed, each passing car sounded like the plumber's truck laboring
up the final hill to our towel-wrapped pipes.
I waited for the engine to die, the door to slam,
the squeak of his tool box as he walked up the path,
someone come to fix things,
                              and my own heavy breaths
became a strange life within me.
I thought it was the baby
                          drowning again,
weak lungs, skin as translucent as butter-stained paper,
my womb, a weak basket
                          filling with water.
I stumbled to the bathroom sink to cool my wrists,
and light from the nursery poured
through the tub's three holes where faucets used to be,
gold light
            as solid as oars in a ship's gunnel
and I thought,
if only someone had explained purgatory this way,
a fevered world,
                  filth and its longing,
I may have believed we could row and row to heaven.

## After the Miscarriage

I try not to think that heaven is memory.
The baby knew nothing
                     but the dark waters
and enveloping sky of my body,
my blood's prattle, the solecisms
of my heart,
            its own heart
pumping the first sips of blood,
its weightless stirring.
Instead I envision the flowers I now tend like children,
how they bend in the wind, even at night
as we make love, the way they sway darkly lit.
But the baby is always there,
imagine, the size of a thumb, swimming,
lit now from within,
                its body glimmering
beneath shiny skin,
the image not of the bloom's sheath
left to dry out, frail and crisp,
but the unsteady flower's head, a ghost,
forever bobbing, dazed above it.

## Mother as Judas

There are two true endings to everything:
Judas, for example, his hanging tree,
his field, bought with blood money;

and my husband's mother, she kissed his sweaty head
one night and slept with a trucker,
because she didn't have the heart

to tell her husband she didn't love him,
or was she in love with what she couldn't have?
It doesn't matter. She's unforgiven.

Yesterday, a woman belted her children
into highchairs and lit gasoline-soaked dishrags.
Love makes us capable of the ugliest sins.

I don't know how to live in this country of mothers;
everywhere I look we sway from branches.
In each yard, a body is bursting open.

## The Pill

For years my body accepted the promise,
the waiting without change, the lie
of a baby taking root, breasts swelling
slightly, never fully, to a tender bruise.
I divided time into little green pills,
popping out one day and then the next,
swallowing my life in measured increments,
and the pink row of sugar pills—
shed blood here—I refused,
closed each case with them rattling
in their plastic bubbles.
Men as bodies not fathers stretched out
before me, breathing destinations on a map.
I envy the woman I was, recklessly
pulling into morning traffic,
blossoms glued by dew wind-plucked gliding up
and over the hood like parade confetti,
the giant Chevy careening like a float.
She would never have seen me, hunched at the wheel,
the brood of children squalling in car seats,
each head a small knot of bones
for me to deliver fully grown to the world,
so like my mother, driving an automatic two-footed,
hitting the gas, the brakes,
and sometimes, I swear, both at once.

## Language Lab, Paris, 1989

Sometimes it comes back to me—
the muffling earphones, plug-charged,
my little half booth—*Elle epluche une orange,*
the words themselves like a thumbnail pressed
into the porous rind, that fine spray.
I tried to repeat with my sloppy American tongue—
hungover, sex-dazed, again and again,
as if one day I could become that silken voice
and marry the French boyfriend
I barely remember now.
I say it aloud still in the simplest moments,
lathering a sliver of soap, stirring pancake batter, never
when peeling an orange; the words
are not their meaning, but if I hold myself there
for a moment I can remember
how my abandoned life had begun, the story
I would have told my French children
if I'd become a French wife
about their mother, young and in love,
the mornings I raced to class, windblown,
red-cheeked, the shop owners unloading trucks,
fish slapped on the St. Denis sidewalk,
the scales shining like a party dress
that slips on as easily as it slips off.
I would say it so perfectly,
*Elle epluche une orange.*

## After Eleven Days of Rain

The woman stolen from her garden
midday has been found, alive.

She has survived in a crack addict's basement,
watching the window wells fill with rain,

the floor weep, the mattress sopping it up.
The sky has broken open.

I don't remember this color blue
although it's lingered, a mute replica,

in the curtain's poppies and dishes' dragonfly trim.
I have stopped hushing the children.

They now run barefoot through the slick grass
as I stumble onto the sun-lit stoop

like Eve, her body a tingling wet rib,
wandering into an orchard of apples.

## The Cow Remembers Urus

Sometimes in the field when her milk well
is full, a white pearl quivers on an udder.

I have seen a drop fall to a blade of grass
and bend it to the dirt. When the children

are asleep, I watch her from their window,
pinbones shifting her hips, her barrel,

the unlocking hock and knee, the balance
on small hooves, her wet delicate dewclaws.

Heart girth, rump, loin, chine,
and beneath the slow rock of her body,

the bob and sway, the nervous tail switches.
Somewhere in the chew and chew of memory,

she remembers her long horns, their white points,
the way she crashed through forests,

driving wolves and bears from bushes,
her voice a wild call from her long throat,

not mournful, but urgent. She did not know
what she was running from or toward. And now

even in winter with the window shut tight,
I can hear her low in the field,

her sweet cry, and the hollow tink of her neck bell
each time she shifts her weight or lifts her heavy head.

## Pharaoh's Dream

I am thinking of Pharaoh's dream of cows eating cows—
how they swam up, wide nostrils and eyes gliding
on the surface like crocodiles, to graze on Nile reeds,

and the bony ones swallowed the fat ones, tails first,
then gulping down ribs—ribs inside ribs—
and no one could recall the healthy girth pitching

over dainty hooves now that there was only a ghostly row
of narrow bones and cupped ears, hungry cows, never full,
living without memory.

        I wonder what will betray me—
the earth, the air, seed or lung. Today is a list:
my chubby daughter shouts red-faced in the hall

for her lost shoes, the garden's earth is full
of wet purple worms, the hooded street lamps
let down rings of light. On the long blue road,

I pass field after field of tall corn. The Egyptians
survived seven years of famine on Joseph's tented grain.
I will never recall this perfect day.

## My Daughter's Sight

Today I saw the nun again
            pulling weeds
in the chapel's flower garden.
Waxy skin has sealed
        her drawn sockets,
and I wonder if I haven't failed you,
                like eyesight,
something you'd come to rely on.
I taught you what I knew
            to be the truth—
our souls are pure,
            evil only a garden snake.
Bit by bit
    colors shifted,
shapes lost their edges,
            particles floated,
retinas detached.
The nun feels each thin stem,
some furred, some leafy, some supple and weak,
and uproots only weeds while
her lips court prayers, her knees in earth
genuflect
        for Jesus, awaiting
his spit and clay;
            I wonder what it feels like
to be the nun, to be you,
to be on the verge of something like sight,
how at first the skin swells,
the new eyes roll and flinch,
and finally rise,
        like teeth,
to fill the living space.

## My Daughter, like Eve, Realizes Nakedness

At graduation, every eighth-grade girl,
dressed in white, walks slowly,

hems swaying as if on boat decks.
I can't find my daughter.

Her jittery gait has changed;
only a month ago, she'd have waved

and whistled through her teeth like a sailor.
I imagine it happened quickly for Eve,

as well, a moment or two of sugary sap,
and then it settled in like a drug

in the blood. (It isn't so simple as an apple,
wagon-red and waxy, the sweet snap in the teeth,

because even the apple knows nakedness,
how, like a miner beneath coal,

the apple is pale when peeled.)
Her body began to burn,

the blush at her neck, her eyes
settling to stare at her feet,

how she began to cave in, the mine again
collapsing in the dark, like my daughter—

I see her now in the poised row—
who even when fully dressed,

knows what the clothes are hiding.
I recognize the hunch of her shoulders,

the hitch in her hips as my own
and remember the wish to unmake myself,

to be a rib again, a perfect white bone
hidden in a row of perfect white bones.

## Cesarean

Once my whole body savored you;
the tight weave of my muscles

and my pelvis's tilted frame
would not give you up.

My belly swelled choke-blue.
I try to envision what it was like:

the dark water world split open,
your body pulled from my body.

This is a well-worn pain,
your backwards birth.

How many times will the world
ask me to repeat it?

And now I watch you lug suitcases
into August's blazing heat.

I imagine your first breath
a sigh, to be not pushed

but finally released, your head eased,
again and again,
from the tight crown of my bones.

# Four

## What the Poets Could Have Been

If every time their minds drifted,
they'd thought instead of a grocery list—
milk, eggs, shoe polish, liniment—
if they could have smelled lemon
and thought of lemons, not their mother's hands,
if they'd been more attentive
to Mr. Twardus's lectures on manliness
while sanding garden boxes in shop class
and more exacting of the apron hem
in Mrs. Niff's home economics,
if they'd been, in some cases, just a little taller
and hadn't fallen so deeply in love each time,
hopping the fence to swim naked with a lover
in the county park pool, their buoyant bodies drifting up
the way words bubble to the mind's surface,
if there were, in general,
less shine, blueness, ticking,
less body and earth, they could have been
repressible, contented. Imagine Hudgins
your minister bent over chapel weeds; Lauterbach
your librarian reading travel books,
pictures of le Tour Eiffel spread open
on her desk; Shapiro your basketball coach,
his thick glasses sliding down his nose
as he calls you off the bench; Levine,
having stuck it out at Detroit Transmission,
now your father's boss, his face
lined hard, eyes squinting.
Imagine if they were your aunts and uncles, tired, smiling
as they drink beer on the back porch—
the simplest things make them happy—

you, for example, twirling your baton up
into the moonlit, mosquito-singing sky,
and all you must do—not this, not words—
is spin and try to catch it
in your unsteady, opening hand.

# Blurbs

I don't want to be *a national treasure,*
too old-codgery, something wheeled out
of a closet to cut ribbon. I prefer
*resident genius,* or for the genius
to be at least *undeniable.*
I'd like to steer away from the declaration
*by far her best.* Too easily I read,
the predecessors were weary immigrant stock.
The same goes for *working at the height*
*of her powers,* as if it's obvious
I'm teetering on the edge of senility.
I don't want to have to look things up:
*lapidary style?* I'd prefer not to be *a talent;*
as if my mother has dressed me
in a spangled leotard, tap shoes,
my hair in Bo-Peep pin curls.
But I like *sexy,* even if unearned.
I like *elegance, bite.* I want someone
to confess they've fallen in love with me
and another to say, *No, she's mine.*
And a third to just come out with it:
*she will go directly to heaven.*

## Dear Mr. Houdini,

We could drown in an inch of water—common knowledge—
a bathtub, a puddle. And we wouldn't come back.
We never pop up from a chained milk barrel like you.
I envy, not how you must have perfected death,
but rebirth,
    how the world must have been shinier
on each return, the light more like dew, the birds fat minnows,
the moon
    like looking down on a pail of milk.
If everyone thinks you're dead, it's like being dead;
so quickly, the giant second-hand turning, you slip
from memory, fade and shrink
        to a hand-held picture in the mind.
It happened to me as a child. Once I got lost on the beach;
I don't remember being found, only the passing rowed hotels,
the brightly striped umbrellas, each woman from a distance
standing hands-on-hips, dark hair wind-tossed like my mother,
each man my father,
      pale-bellied, hunched and hairless,
and how it felt to disappear.
I don't want to hear that you laid down in the coffin
and breathed quietly,
      of the coughed-up keys, dislocated joints,
the way you lived on your own air.
I want a trick, magic,
        because life would be so easy.
I could die and then bob to the surface like a ripened berry.
Damn, I could say I was the sailor's mooring star
and for once mean something.

## The Assumption: Mary's Heart in the *Guinness Book of World Records*

> . . . his mother kept all these things in her heart.
> —LUKE 2:51

They can barely lift her
                    off the ground—imagine Kitty Hawk,
that noisy winged machine
                    nose-tipping from land,
the engine's stutter-punch.
There's a team of angels, sent for the regalia,
but each necessary now
                    to haul her into heaven,
each groaning, red-cheeked
in a tug-of-war
                    against gravity and, of course,
her obese heart.
It outweighs the tumor removed from a woman's ovary
in California, 303 pounds,
                    wheeled out on its own stretcher;
but no reporter is here
                    to heft it onto a scale,
scribble a note, snap a bright poof of photo-flash.
We know it holds the record, how it began
                    a hard red apple,
clicking,
        then she said yes
                    to the angel, the child,
and her heart became a pocket, swelled to the size
of a purse, a suitcase, a steamer trunk,
                    fed a steady diet
of sorrow
        and things unsaid.

And the beating grew loud, the constant rush
                                    of blood, and pounding, until,
in the end,
            nothing could be heard
above her roaring heart.

## What I Told the Jehovah's Witness

When I was a kid, my grandfather put on his hat and died.
Two days later a local woman drowned in a shallow cranberry bog.
I avoided hats and cranberries and eventually
anything to do with Pilgrims, who seemed fond of both.
I started praying
                    to the neighbor's bird-stained statue
of St. Francis. See how religions start up with misconnected
brain fuses?
            You say everything bad is getting worse,
the world is a wormy apple, that my neighbors are sick and dying.
But look at your red ears, straight teeth, that Adam's apple bobbing
at your starched collar, such a sweet boy with a briefcase of Bibles.
Someone raised you in the artificial glow
                            of the fifties,
neon crap, as if some golden age has passed
—just ask Mr. Jackson in 4F about that scar
on his forehead from the billy club,
and the Middle Ages, I hear,
                    were no joyride.
I once skimmed the Statistical Abstract, looked up death,
not the penalty, not the variously typical diseases,
but weather-related:
Fires in Southern California, deaths, 9.
Hurricane in Florida and Louisiana, deaths, 4.
I let my finger glide down the chart,
and I knew how the world would end
like the summer of '88 when I was young
and fucking sweetly
                    and every day was as bright
as your pretty cartoon pamphlet of drowsy lions and lambs,
how people died by the thousands from Heatwave/Drought,
how we will die not from what we fear
—hats and cranberries and Pilgrims—
but under persistent blue skies, sunshine.

## Discussing Sorrow with Jesus

The blood blurs his vision
        so he's always winking
like a diner waitress, eye-teared
by her cigarette's smoke,
        and I ask to take his hat
—thorns, really—but no, he says, I'm fine.
It's so like him,
        to suffer openly,
and I tell him,
        It's too much,
the way your whittled shape
        still dangles
from gold chains and rearview mirrors
tangled in wedding garters,
        hung forever
on the back wall of Verbitski's fish shop.
You said that we would forget
        the sorrow
after your resurrection, like a woman forgets labor
once the child is born.
        But we haven't forgotten.
And it's a poor metaphor,
because women do not forget,
        our bodies ripped open,
the knowledge that life simply passes through,
that the child isn't born
        but taken
and we had thought it a gift.
No, each time, a woman resigns herself to joy,
like choosing
        the bruised and bitten fruit
because the bin is almost empty.

But I've gone too far, he's embarrassed now,
slouching, arms crossed
                    to hide the wound
in his side, his hands' nail holes;
and legs crossed to cover
                    his soft penis.
Tired now,
        he lies down on the sofa.
Only to rest his eyes, he says,
and I cover him
            with a white sheet
that I know he will stain as he sleeps
                        like a young girl
who bleeds without knowing, and I watch as the blood inches
like brilliant red night-crawling spores,
covering the white until it is not his body,
                        but his image,
a perfect blood-stiffened cast of our Lord
and beneath it his shallow breathing.

# My Cousin Attempts Suicide in Gander Hill Prison

Today in solitary, stripped-down,
he bashed his head
                    against the cell wall
until there was a risen welt and blood.
The guard gave him an ice pack;
once alone, he tore it open
                    and drank
the thick blue liquid. My mother calls to tell the story
and quickly changes the subject, complains
about the cornfield newly cut
                    to stubble
and how the mice pour
                    into the old farmhouse
like water
            through each small crack.
Even a farmhouse can leak
                    and sink
into dry earth. She says, *Nothing is watertight.*
I agree, *Some things are out of our hands.*
It feels good to say, but isn't entirely true.
I remember how as a boy in summer,
                                    he never cupped
the lightning bugs, hands match-lit,
but smeared
            their bodies' electric oil
on his bare chest, his arms,
                    how he ran
through the tall corn,
calling to us before stepping out
                            into the yard,
before standing—arms wide, howling—
like a leper
            with glorious glowing wounds.

## Jesus in the Mail

Someone at the Shrine of Divine Mercy
knows I'm a lapsed Catholic;
a card comes in the mail; a chapelful of nuns
(I'd prefer a nun full of chapels)

is offering the perpetual novena, celebrated daily.
There's a checklist of spiritual ailments.
I pause over *lukewarm souls* and *those
who separated themselves from His body.*

I didn't know the soul was temperate,
made of water; and his body, I'd never thought
of myself as attached. And yet now
both seem right, and I imagine

the soul poured into unknotted ribs,
that we are bodies of water, and I hope
that death, when it comes, will feel like
what it was to be a girl back-floating on a lake,

pulling down armfuls, then gliding,
arms outstretched and rowing
like Christ coming out of his own body,
flying from the heavy cross.

## On My Husband's Thirty-Third Birthday

The Filipino woman—two doors down—
with one arm shrunken to the bone
survived the Death March on cans
of food stolen from MacArthur's kitchen.
There, she'd smelled the American brand

of heaven: fine white bubbles
perched around the pitcher's curved edge,
white swirls in ham, all the meat
coming so easily off the bone,
the way words in a foreign language

release themselves from meaning
and dissolve on the tongue.
And when the General did not return
as promised—aren't we all weary
of waiting?—the food turned rusty, gray.

Don't take survival tips from Jesus.
He's a sorry role model, so thin
you'd think he'd have died of starvation
if not for the angry mob, the cross,
his inability to cheat the truth.

She advises, when the drunk Japanese soldiers
come for you at night, if you shake
and chant *malaria, malaria,*
they will not rape you. She says,
*If you are shot but not dead, play dead.*

## Living Where They Raised Me

Delaware is ripe with cancer—
its shallow fields and factories without run-off,
but we don't speak of it, the hometowners,
because we aren't going anywhere.
From here, Ohio sounds exotic.
But we wonder how it will settle in,
where the curdled cells will take root.
In school, I was impressed
by the filmstrip of the woman born armless,
who could do everything with her feet—
trim her son's bangs, swat flies,
stir cake batter with her rump on the counter,
one leg around the bowl,
a wooden spoon hooked in her toes.
A nervous child, I prepared,
practiced the barefoot art
of turning pages, scrawling my name.
But my arms never fell off.
In fact, they are still here,
my feet still holding ground,
my pink organs turning this into that,
and Delaware, surrounded by the rumor
of mountains, is still flat,
its back unbroken, refusing to attempt
that sort of useless resurrection.
It's easy to blame the land,
to think if we lived somewhere else—
Hackensack or Damascus—
believing would be so easy.

## The Beginning

My grandfather can taste words now.
They linger in his mouth,
swell on his tongue,
*thimble, horn, flask, fedora.*

Each a sweet fruit cut into wedges,
they fit perfectly in his mouth.
He doesn't know that when he speaks
the words grow heavy, hoofed, rooted.

My mother and I sit on the floor of his bedroom closet,
sorting letters gone yellow.
*Chrome, liver, weather, fish.*
The baby kicks inside my womb,

and she says she can feel it in her own,
the tremors of memory.
*Coalmine, hemline, parsnip, hive.*
Sometimes death begins in the mouth,

within the tongue and lips,
*root, hum, quiver, stitch.*
It begins simply: the word comes
and nothing follows, no heat,

no gleam, no breath or blueness,
slowly you are released,
*husk, glow, window, rib,*
a word without this ugly body.

# The Dead Must Disappear or Join a Story

*for my grandfather, Glen*

Memory can work this way
like the man in the Old Testament
thrown into the common plot;
his body touched Elijah's bones,
and he stood in his grave,
climbed up from the pit
into the middle of a brawl.
I wonder if he dreamed forever after
of mingling sweetly with the earth,
of clean memory.
Did he want to be brought back?
Do you?
            I want you to dance
and you dance like a foal, knees buckling,
until your face is red and pulsing
like a giant heart.
                        You will get used to it,
these constant resurrections,
this enormous new body
you've swelled into, and the living,
the way we will tell everything
to anyone
willing to touch our burning skin.

# Five

## My Mother among Bears

Dressed in slacks, jacket,
chained half-glasses perched
on her powdered bosom
to inspect foliage, my mother
meets a black bear
on her morning path, its long hair
sunlit, its breath rising.
Unafraid, she bellows—the way she shouts
at foreign cabbies and lispy waiters—
*I'm old!* This the bear knows,
he sniffs the air, no iron scent
of blood gathers between her legs.
Close enough to winter, their bodies
are slowing alike. They spend the day,
sipping webs heavy with dew,
rolling berries juice-tight
across their tongues. At dusk,
she picks clean the clan's
giant teeth with minty
cellophane-packaged toothpicks
found in her purse pockets.
She scrubs coats while claws soak
in lemon water and schools the cubs
in manners, how to politely bone a fish.
But as she tries to sleep, curled up
to a warm fur belly, she imagines us,
long-toothed and lonely, weeping away
our blood. *Who will bathe their souls?*
she wonders. *Who will remind them*
*to eat liver, ginger, evening primrose?*
She's right. Look at us, naked and stupid,
running wildly with sticks.

## My Mother Prays to Dream of Her Dead Father

But when she finally pulls over
                          at the seedy roadside carnival,
stumbles past the giant clicking numbered wheel,
                                 the swayback pony,
the eight-legged calf, and she finds him,
                            dipping up beet borscht
in an oil-stained apron, *My god,* she says,
                          *What are you doing here?,*
forgetting it was her will. And what did she expect?
A pearled gate
              with auto-trumpet, a tailored
tunic, and twenty-four-hour harp over intercom?
Then she figures he's paying a debt;
                     he was never perfect
even after eulogy upon eulogy
                    meant to starch and press
his soul; she can still recall
his extravagant failures, her mother's bruised arms,
the silence he held
              like a fist in his mouth.
His purgatory now is shabby carnivals,
motor vehicle lines, bus stops,
                 this human world
that he'd always thought beneath him.
But this is a dream of the living,
            not a reality,
she reminds herself later sipping coffee alone
at the sink,
        that it's her sins she's come to claim,
that for years he will ladle borscht,
weep into the salty broth, and heaven,

when it finally arrives, will be a stretch of beach,
a dream
     of her father, this time holding a golden
gold-eyed fish above his sun-haloed head.

# My Mother in the Garden

She pauses over the spring flowers that give in
to the heat,
        the marigolds' faded yellow
settled to soft webbing, the tulips' petals turned crisp,
fallen, their proud green stems, pursed lips
that whiten and shrink.
               She asks me
why we choose red over brown, taut
over shriveled.
*See the beautiful folds of skin?*
The rhododendrons' blossoms slide, sometimes,
down the stamen, still purple, intact.
*And if you are patient,* she says,
*you will see the stamen*
            *curl toward heaven, the bloom*
*will lift its frail brown skirts, girlishly,*
*and let them fall, at last,*
        *to the wanting ground.*

## Mummification

This is the way I will
so lovingly
            stuff your body with earth,
bones cord-wrapped, skin
painted with ash paste,
a bird-skin cap
stitched
            with my own hair
and a cactus needle.
I will not be outdone
by Chinchurros.
You have taught me
how to haul
my love around
                  on my back,
hunched from solid weight,
how it becomes
a comfort to bear. And, yes,
I will tilt your mouth
open, remembering how much
you love to sing.

## The Extra Rib

I worry that it's calcified cancer
poking oddly from my back,
but the doctor says it's an extra rung
at the bottom of the rib cage,
a genetic freebie, like the bones
beneath my tongue
that the dentist said most humans
have abandoned in evolution.
My mother, he joked, drank too much milk.
I am prehistoric, an Adam, the ache
of language lingers in mouth bones
and body cage. I am afraid
to fall asleep in this sooty Eden,
wondering if God will start it all again
with this extra rib,
a bit of mud and breath.
What could lie beyond these gates?

CRAB ORCHARD AWARD SERIES IN POETRY

*In Search of the Great Dead*
Richard Cecil

*Names above House*
Oliver de la Paz

*The Star-Spangled Banner*
Denise Duhamel

*Winter Amnesties*
Elton Glaser

*Crossroads and Unholy Water*
Marilene Phipps

*Misery Prefigured*
J. Allyn Rosser